MISSION

RETHINKING VOCATION

MISSION

RETHINKING VOCATION

BY JOHN STOTT

From *Christian Mission in the Modern World*

FOREWORD BY STEVEN GARBER

REGENT COLLEGE PUBLISHING
Vancouver, British Columbia

M. J. MURDOCK CHARITABLE TRUST
Vancouver, Washington

INTRODUCTION
STEVEN GARBER

The Challenge

I was in Nashville recently, and one morning had breakfast with two men—a musician whom I have known for many years and a physician. They live on the same block, and spend their days loving their wives and children even as they love the city and the world. They wanted to talk about vocation.

So over muffins and cups of tea we talked about their lives and loves. Thoughtful folk, they read widely and care deeply, enough so to write me a few months earlier asking to talk sometime about something that mattered to them. In so many ways the conversation was familiar to me, even as it was uniquely situated within their experiences of family, education, community, work, and church.

When we got up from the table, the physician, a Nashville dermatologist, said, "If what you are saying is true, then it changes everything, you know?" I do know that, and I will not forget his words. If we see ourselves as called into the world, having a vocation from God that makes sense of everything that we are—even seeing through a glass darkly as we do at our best—then it changes the way we see what we do. He saw that having a word like "vocation" would change the way he understands the relationship of worship to work, of what he believes to the way he lives.

He is a kind man, a gifted man, an astute man, and yet he still longs for something more, namely, to see the stuff of his life integrally woven into the truest truths of the universe. In a word, he wants to see that his work matters to God and to the world. Not principally because he makes money so that others can do work that is important to God; rather that his work as a physician is integrally part of the work God is doing in history.

But why is this man at 38 only now finding his way into the word "vocation"? As an undergraduate, he was part of a highly regarded campus ministry, and as an adult, he has faithfully participated in a church where God is honored, where the Bible is believed to be true, and where the needs of the city and the world are central to the congregational mission. And yet, his words were, "If what you are saying is true, then it changes everything."

The Vision of Vocation in the Vision of John Stott

A generation ago now, John Stott, perhaps the most widely respected pastoral and theological voice in Protestantism throughout the world, gave a series of lectures at Oxford University. Published as *Christian Mission in the Modern World*, Stott took up five words, lecturing on each. The first word was "mission."

INTRODUCTION

In the long line of his good gifts to the Church, Stott offers his unusual ability to think clearly about complex questions, exploring the meaning of "mission," biblically and theologically. Arguing that Christ explicitly made his mission the model for ours, Stott develops the anthropological and missiological heart of the mission of Christ, resisting every attempt to bifurcate the work of God in the world, making some things "sacred" and others "secular," some parts of life what God cares about and other parts of life what he does not care about—at least as much. Necessarily then, he deeply resists every effort to create a tension between evangelism and social responsibility, namely, which matters more to God, and therefore ought to matter more to us? Because we are a "body-soul-in community," and not only a "soul," Stott maintains that the mission of Christ addresses the complexity of the human condition, with its rich anthropological vision, all of life addressed by all of the gospel.

After this serious examination of the mission of Christ, the final section is called, "Practical Implications," where Stott says, "We must then begin with vocation," and therefore repent of the unbiblical hierarchy that the Church has taught so widely and well for most of its history. Hierarchy? He argues that we have taught that some callings are more important than others, that some work is, truth to be told, more central to the mission of Christ. For example, that an overseas missionary is the most prized of all vocations, that a pastor at home is next, that those in the helping professions are next . . . and all the way down to the bottom of the list where the politicians are found!

Everything about God, about his work in the world through the life, death and resurrection of Christ, about the human condition and history, is an argument against this hierarchy, Stott believes. And we should too.

Why don't we? Why is it that we are still stumbling over this? Why is it that we do not see our calling as salt and light—"affecting our environments" as Stott argues—and so rather than cursing the darkness of our communities and world, seeing that it is our responsibility to light candles, with humility, grace and courage showing what human flourishing longs for and requires? Or rather than blaming the decay of our world on the world, taking the responsibility that is ours to salt the earth, stopping the decay in and through our vocations and occupations? Why is it that we do not understand the whole gospel for the whole person in the whole world—and therefore understand that vocation is integral, not incidental, to the mission of God?

A few years ago I spoke at a men's retreat on this theme of vocation. After the final session, several men came up to me and said that they had brought an English friend with them who had something important to say about what he had heard.

> I am 50 years old and have been in the Church my whole life. My work has been at the intersection of business and technology, but over the years I have come to the conclusion that work like I do is "second-class" work. That if I had been more serious, more visionary, I would have done something that God would have been honored by, something more "religious" than what I

> have done with my life. But I want to tell you that over
> the weekend a wound in my heart has been healed.

A generation after Stott gave his lecture, the Church needs ears to hear. There are wounds in the hearts of men and women all over the world, people like the musician and physician in Nashville—and this man at the conference – who are members of good churches pastored by good people, but where the vision of vocation is not an integral part of the liturgical life of the congregation, nor is it seen as an integral part of the mission of the congregation.

The Bible's teaching, and Stott's articulation of it is that vocation is integral, not incidental, to the mission of God, to the *missio Dei*, to the work of God in history. What is taught instead is that what God is doing in the world is above and beyond, and sadly, indifferent, to what most people spend most of their lives doing; it is what we do in the "off" hours of Sunday and after work where the work of God is done. Most times in most places the Church still stumbles over this, teaching by word and deed that vocation is incidental, not integral, to the mission of God, leaving folk like the man at the conference with a wound in his heart, sure that his choice to work in the marketplace of the world is "second-class."

Why All This Matters

In December 2010, the Murdock Trust and the Stewardship Foundation co-sponsored the annual Leadership Advance, a gathering of leaders from throughout the Pacific Northwest. I gave the first plenary presentation, "Why All This Matters," in which I explored the vision of "common grace for the common good," and the ways that the work of Jack Murdock and Davis Weyerhauser were important examples of that in their businesses in technology and timber.

The next day a group of men came up to me, saying, "We have been talking about what you said for a day now. We ourselves have been in business, and we have lived for years with the burden of our work as "blood money," that it was only important because it gave us the ability to now give money away. Seeing our lives that way has never been satisfying. How did you begin to think the way you do, where everything is coherent, where it all matters?"

We sat down over lunch later that day and talked. I told them that the teaching of Stott has been crucial to me, giving me eyes to see that the mission of Christ must shape my mission, that the work of God addresses the world made by God—in all its complexity and wonder, sorrow and grief—full as it is of good work to be done by butchers and bakers and candlestick-makers, salt and light each one, affecting their places in the world by bringing the good news of the kingdom into the ordinary places of ordinary people. At home and in neighborhoods, but also in the worlds of education, business, politics, medicine, law, the arts, and on and on. We are not called to curse the world for being the world; rather we are to ask, "Why didn't we act as salt and light, penetrating the world in and through our vocations?" That is the mission of Christ, and simply said, it is our mission.

MISSION

JOHN STOTT

The first word we have to consider is *mission*. Before attempting a biblical definition, it may be helpful to take a look at the contemporary polarization.

Two Extreme Views

The older or traditional view has been to equate mission and evangelism, missionaries and evangelists, missions and evangelistic programs. Even the Commission on World Mission and Evangelism did not distinguish in its constitution between "mission" and "evangelism," but defined its aim as "to further the proclamation to the whole world of the gospel of Jesus Christ, to the end that all men may believe in him and be saved." As Philip Potter said in his address to the World Council of Churches (WCC) Central Committee meeting in Crete in 1967, "ecumenical literature since Amsterdam has used 'mission,' 'witness' and 'evangelism' interchangeably."

In its extreme form, this older view of mission as consisting exclusively of evangelism also concentrated on verbal proclamation. The missionary was often caricatured as standing under a palm tree, wearing a sola topi, and declaiming the gospel to a group of ill-clad natives sitting respectfully round him on the ground. Thus the traditional image of the missionary was of the preacher, and a rather paternalistic kind of preacher at that. Such an emphasis on the priority of evangelistic preaching left little room in some cases even for the founding of Christian schools. Philip Crowe told us at the 1968 Islington Conference of a certain R. N. Cust who argued in 1888 that missionary money "was collected for the purpose of converting a soul, not sharpening an intellect." He slightly modified his position in 1894 to include "a lay evangelist, a female evangelist, a medical evangelist whenever gospel preaching is the substantive work," but added: "when it is proposed to have a pious industrial superintendent, or an evangelical tile manufacturer, or a low church breeder of cattle or raiser of turnips, I draw my line" (*Mission in the Modern World*, Patmos, 1968).

This is a very extreme example, however. Most adherents of the traditional view of mission would regard education and medical work as perfectly proper, and indeed as very useful adjuncts to evangelistic work, often out of Christian compassion for the ignorant and the sick, though sometimes as being unashamedly "platforms" or "springboards" for evangelism—hospitals and schools providing in their patients and pupils a conveniently captive audience for the gospel. In either case, the mission itself was understood in terms of evangelism.

This traditional view is far from being dead and buried. The so-called Jesus movement has encouraged the formation of Christian communes into which zealous young evangelicals withdraw from the wicked world. For a commune easily degenerates into a compound, and even into a quasimonastic establishment. Then the only contact which such Christians have with the world (which they regard as totally and irredeemably wicked) is to make occasional evangelistic raids into it. Apocalyptic imagery comes natural to them. The world is like a building on fire, they say; a Christian's only duty is to mount a rescue operation before it is too late. Jesus Christ is coming at any moment; there is no point in tampering with the structures of society, for society is doomed and about to be destroyed.

Besides, any attempt to improve society is bound to be unproductive, since unrenewed men cannot build a new world. Man's only hope lies in being born again. Only then might society conceivably be reborn. But it is too late now even for that.

Such world-denying pessimism is a strange phenomenon in those who say they believe in God. But then their image of God is only partially shaped by the biblical revelation. He is not the Creator who in the beginning gave man a "cultural mandate" to subdue and rule the earth, who has instituted governing authorities as his "ministers" to order society and maintain justice, and who, as the Lausanne Covenant puts it, because he is "both the

Creator and the Judge of all men" is concerned for "justice and reconciliation throughout human society" (para. 5).

At the opposite extreme of this unbiblical concept of mission as consisting of evangelism alone there is the standard ecumenical viewpoint, at least since the middle 1960s and the preparatory work for the Uppsala Assembly.

The publication in 1967 of the reports of the Western European and North American working groups on "the missionary structure of the congregation," titled *The Church for Others* (WCC), gave currency to a whole new vocabulary of mission. The thesis developed in these reports was that God is at work in the historical process, that the purpose of his mission,of the *missio Dei*, is the establishment of *shalom* (Hebrew for "peace") in the sense of social harmony, and that this *shalom* (which it was suggested is identical with the kingdom of God) is exemplified in "the emancipation of coloured races, the concern for the humanization of industrial relations, various attempts at rural development, the quest for business and professional ethics, the concern for intellectual honesty and integrity" (*The Church for Others*, p. 15).

Moreover, in working toward this goal, God uses "men and women both inside and outside the churches," and the church's particular role in the mission of God is to "point to God at work in world history" (p. 16), to discover what he is doing, to catch up with it and to get involved in it ourselves. For God's primary relationship is to the world, it was argued, so that the true sequence is to be found no longer in the formula "God-church-world" but in the formula "God-world-church" (p. 16). This being so, "it is the world that must

be allowed to provide the agenda for the churches" (p. 20)—
the churches taking the world seriously and seeking to serve
according to its contemporary sociological needs.

Professor J. G. Davies, who had been a member of the
West European working group, expressed similar ideas in his
two books *Worship and Mission* (SCM, 1966) and *Dialogue
with the World* (SCM, 1967). He equated humanization, reconciliation, shalom and the setting up of God's kingdom
as being together the goal of mission (*Dialogue*, pp. 12-16).
"Hence mission is concerned with the overcoming of industrial disputes, with the surmounting of class divisions, with
the eradication of racial discrimination" (p. 14). Indeed, "we
are required to enter into partnership with God in history to
renew society" (p. 15).

Much of this attempted reconstruction of 'mission' was
quoted in the *Drafts for Sections*, which were published in
preparation for Uppsala. Mission was seen as the historical process of the renewal of society, and the theme text of
Uppsala was "Behold, I make all things new" (Revelation
21:5). But this word of God is an eschatological affirmation. It
is uttered from the throne (in John's vision) almost immedi-
ately after the new heaven and the new earth have appeared.
Yet several times at Uppsala it was used as an expression not
of future hope but of present reality, not of the final regen-
eration of the universe but of "the acceleration of social and
political change."

Apart from this misuse of Scripture, what are we to say
about the identification of the mission of God with social
renewal? A fourfold critique may be made. First, the God who

is Lord of history is also the Judge of history. It is naive to hail all revolutionary movements as signs of divine renewal. After the revolution, the new status quo sometimes enshrines more injustice and oppression than the one it has displaced.

Second, the biblical categories of *shalom*, the new humanity and the kingdom of God are not to be identified with social renewal. It is true that in the Old Testament *shalom* (peace) often indicates political and material well-being. But can it be maintained, as serious biblical exegesis, that the New Testament authors present Jesus Christ as winning this kind of peace and as bestowing it on society as a whole? To assume that all Old Testament prophecies are fulfilled in literal and material terms is to make the very mistake which Jesus' contemporaries made when they tried to take him by force and make him a king (John 6:15).

The New Testament understanding of Old Testament prophecy is that its fulfillment *transcends* the categories in which the promises were given. So according to the apostles the peace which Jesus preaches and gives is something deeper and richer, namely, reconciliation and fellowship with God and with each other (e.g., Ephesians 2:13-22). Moreover, he does not bestow it on all men but on those who belong to him, to his redeemed community. So *shalom* is the blessing the Messiah brings to his people. The new creation and the new humanity are to be seen in those who are in Christ (2 Corinthians 5:17); and the kingdom has to be received like a little child (Mark 10:15). Certainly it is our Christian duty to commend by argument and example the righteous standards of the kingdom to those who have not themselves received or entered it. In this way we see the righteousness of the kingdom, as it were, "spilling over" into segments of the world and thus to some extent blurring the frontiers between the two. Nevertheless the kingdom remains distinct from godless society, and actual entry into it depends on spiritual rebirth.

Third, the word *mission* cannot properly be used to cover everything God is doing in the world. In providence and common grace he is indeed active in all men and all societies, whether they acknowledge him or not. But this is not his "mission." "Mission" concerns his redeemed people and what he sends *them* into the world to do.

Fourth, Uppsala's preoccupation with social change left little or no room for evangelistic concern. It was this imbalance against which, if I may speak personally, I felt I had to protest at the plenary session at which the report of Section 2, "Renewal in Mission," was made.

"The Assembly has given its earnest attention to the hunger, poverty and injustices of the contemporary world," I said. "Rightly so. I have myself been moved by it. But I do not find a comparable concern or compassion for the spiritual hunger of men. . . . The church's first priority . . . remains the millions and millions . . . who (as Christ and his apostles tell us again and again) being without Christ are perishing. . . . The World Council of Churches professes to acknowledge Jesus Christ as Lord. Well, the Lord Jesus Christ sent his church to preach the good news and make disciples; I do not see this Assembly as a whole eager to obey his command. The Lord Jesus Christ wept over the impenitent city which had rejected him; I do not see this Assembly weeping any similar tears."

A Biblical Synthesis?

From the traditional view of mission as exclusively evangelistic and the current ecumenical view of it as the establishment of *shalom*, we ask if there is a better way, a more balanced and more biblical way of defining the mission of the church, and of relating to one another the evangelistic and social responsibilities of the people of God. The delegates to the meeting of the Commission on World Mission and Evangelism in Mexico City in December 1963 saw the problem, but said they were unable to find a solution. They confessed in the report of Section 3:

> Debate returned again and again to the relationship between God's action in and through the Church and everything God is doing in the world apparently independently of the Christian community. Can a distinction be drawn between God's providential action and God's redeeming action? . . . We were able to state thesis and antithesis in this debate, but we could not see our way through to the truth which we feel lies beyond this dialectic. (*Witness in Six Continents*, edited by R. K. Orchard, Edinburgh House Press, 1964, p. 157).

Many came to Uppsala hoping for a genuine meeting of minds by which this tension could be resolved. In one of the opening speeches, Dr. W. A. Visser 't Hooft expressed the hope that the Assembly would deal with this issue "positively and ecumenically"—"positively in the sense that we give a clear sense of orientation to our movement" and "ecumeni-

cally in the sense that we will truly listen to each other." He
went on to make his own contribution by saying:

> I believe that, with regard to the great tension between
> the vertical interpretation of the Gospel as essentially
> concerned with God's saving action in the life of
> individuals, and the horizontal interpretation of it as
> mainly concerned with human relationships in the
> world, we must get out of that rather primitive oscillat-
> ing movement of going from one extreme to the other,
> which is not worthy of a movement which by its nature
> seeks to embrace the truth of the gospel in its fulness.
> A Christianity which has lost its vertical dimension has
> lost its salt and is not only insipid in itself, but useless
> for the world. But a Christianity which would use the
> vertical preoccupation as a means to escape from its
> responsibility for and in the common life of man is a
> denial of the incarnation, of God's love for the world
> manifested in Christ. (*The Uppsala 68 Report*, edited
> by Norman Goodall, WCC, Geneva, 1968, pp. 317-18)

But unfortunately what Mexico left unfinished Uppsala
did not complete, and Dr. Visser 't Hooft's hope was unful-
filled. The old polarization continues.

All of us should be able to agree that mission arises
primarily out of the nature not of the church but of God
himself. The living God of the Bible is a sending God. I think
it was Johannes Blauw in his book *The Missionary Nature
of the Church* (1962) who first used the word centrifugal to
describe the church's mission. Then Professor J. G. Davies
applied it to God himself. God, he writes, is "a centrifugal
Being" (*Worship and Mission*, 1966, p. 28). It is a dramatic

figure of speech. Yet it is only another way of saying that God is love, always reaching out after others in self-giving service.

So he sent forth Abraham, commanding him to go from his country and kindred into the great unknown, and promising to bless him and to bless the world through him if he obeyed (Genesis 12:1-3). Next, he sent Joseph into Egypt, overruling even his brothers' cruelty, in order to preserve a godly remnant on earth during the famine (Genesis 45:4-8). Then he sent Moses to his oppressed people in Egypt with good news of liberation, saying to him: "Come, I will send you to Pharaoh that you may bring forth my people . . . out of Egypt" (Exodus 3:10). After the exodus and the settlement, he sent a continuous succession of prophets with words of warning and of promise to his people. As he said through Jeremiah, "From the day that your fathers came out of the land of Egypt to this day, I have persistently sent all my servants the prophets to them, day after day, yet they did not listen to me" (Jeremiah 7:25-26; cf. 2 Chronicles 36:15-16). After the Babylonian captivity he graciously sent them back to the land, and sent more messengers with them and to them to help them rebuild the temple, the city and the national life. Then at last "when the time had fully come, God sent forth his Son," and after that the Father and the Son sent forth the Spirit on the day of Pentecost (Galatians 4:4-6; John 14:26; 15:26; 16:7; Acts 2:33).

All this is the essential biblical background to any under-standing of mission. The primal mission is God's, for it is he who sent his prophets, his Son, his Spirit. Of these missions the mission of the Son is central, for it was the culmination of the ministry of the prophets, and it embraced within itself as its climax the sending of the Spirit. And now the Son sends as he himself was sent. Already during his public ministry he sent out first the apostles and then the seventy as a kind of extension of his own preaching, teaching and healing ministry. After his death and resurrection, he widened the scope of the mission to include all who call him Lord and themselves his disciples, for others were present with the Twelve when the Great Commission was given (e.g., Luke 24:33); we cannot restrict its application to the apostles.

The Great Commission

This brings us to a consideration of the terms of the Great Commission. What was it that the Lord Jesus commissioned his people to do? There can be no doubt that most versions of it (for he seems to have repeated it in several forms on several occasions) place the emphasis on evangelism. "Go into all the world and preach the gospel to the whole creation" is the familiar command of the "longer ending" of Mark's Gospel which seems to have been added by some later hand after Mark's original conclusion was lost (Mark 16:15). "Go . . . and make disciples of all nations, baptizing them . . . and teaching them" is the Matthean form (Matthew 28:19-20), while Luke records at the end of his Gospel Christ's word "that repentance and forgiveness of sins should be preached in his name to all nations" and at the beginning of the Acts that his people would receive power to become his witnesses to the end of the earth (Luke 24:47; Acts 1:8). The cumulative emphasis seems clear. It is placed on preaching, witnessing and making disciples, and many deduce from this that the mission of the church, according to the specification of the risen Lord, is exclusively a preaching, converting and teaching mission. Indeed, I confess that I myself argued this at the World Congress on Evangelism in Berlin in 1966, when attempting to expound the three major versions of the Great Commission.

Today, however, I would express myself differently. It is not just that the Commission includes a duty to teach converts everything Jesus had previously commanded (Matthew 28:20), and that social responsibility is among the things which Jesus commanded. I now see more clearly that not only the consequences of the Commission but the actual Commission itself must be understood to include social as well as evangelistic responsibility, unless we are to be guilty of distorting the words of Jesus.

The crucial form in which the Great Commission has been handed down to us (though it is the most neglected because it is the most costly) is the Johannine. Jesus had anticipated it in his prayer in the upper room when he said to the Father: "As thou didst send me into the world, so I have sent them into world" (John 17:18). Now, probably in the same upper room but after his death and resurrection, he turned his prayer-statement into a commission and said: "As the Father has sent me, even so I send you" (John 20:21). In both these sentences Jesus did more than draw a vague parallel between his mission and ours. Deliberately and precisely he made his mission the *model* of ours, saying "as the Father has sent me, even so I send you." Therefore our understanding of the church's mission must be deduced from our understanding of the Son's. Why and how did the Father send the Son?

Of course the major purpose of the Son's coming into the world was unique. Perhaps it is partly for this reason that Christians have been hesitant to think of their mission as in any sense comparable to his. For the Father sent the Son to be the Savior of the world, and to that end to atone for our sins and to bring us eternal life (1 John 4:9-10, 14). Indeed, he himself said he had come "to seek and to save the lost" (Luke 19:10). We cannot copy him in these things. We are not saviors. Nevertheless, all this is still an inadequate statement of why he came.

It is better to begin with something more general and say that he came to serve. His contemporaries were familiar with Daniel's apocalyptic vision of the son of man receiving dominion and being served by all peoples (Daniel 7:14). But Jesus knew he had to serve before he would be served, and to endure suffering before he would receive dominion. So he fused two apparently incompatible Old Testament images, Daniel's son of man and Isaiah's suffering servant, and said: "the Son of man . . . came not to be served but to serve, and to give his life a ransom for many" (Mark 10:45).

The ransoming sin-offering was a sacrifice which he alone could offer, but this was to be the climax of a life of service, and we too may serve. "I am among you," he said on another occasion, "as one who serves" (Luke 22:27). So he gave himself in selfless service for others, and his service took a wide variety of forms according to men's needs. Certainly he preached, proclaiming the good news of the kingdom of

God and teaching about the coming and the nature of the kingdom, how to enter it and how it would spread. But he served in deed as well as in word, and it would be impossible in the ministry of Jesus to separate his works from his words. He fed hungry mouths and washed dirty feet, he healed the sick, comforted the sad and even restored the dead to life.

Now he sends us, he says, as the Father had sent him. Therefore our mission, like his, is to be one of service. He emptied himself of status and took the form of a servant, and his humble mind is to be in us (Philippians 2:5-8). He supplies us with the perfect model of service and sends his church into the world to be a servant church. Is it not essential for us to recover this biblical emphasis? In many of our Christian attitudes and enterprises we have tended (especially those of us who live in Europe and North America) to be rather bosses than servants. Yet it seems that it is in our servant role that we can find the right synthesis of evangelism and social action. For both should be for us, as they undoubtedly were for Christ, authentic expressions of the love that serves.

Then there is another aspect of the mission of the Son which is to be paralleled in the mission of the church, namely, that in order to serve he was sent *into the world.* He did not touch down like a visitor from outer space, or arrive like an alien bringing his own alien culture with him. He took to himself our humanity, our flesh and blood, our culture. He actually became one of us and experienced our frailty, our suffering and our temptations. He even bore our sin and died our death. And now he sends us "into the world," to identify with others as he identified with us (though without losing our Christian identity), to become vulnerable as he did. It is surely one of the most characteristic failures of us Christians, not least of us who are called evangelical Christians, that we seldom seem to take seriously this principle of the incarnation. "As our Lord took on our flesh," runs the report from Mexico City 1963, "so he calls his Church to take on the secular world. This is easy to say and sacrificial to do" (*Witness in Six Continents*, p. 151). It comes more natural to us to shout the gospel at people from a distance than to involve ourselves deeply in their lives, to think ourselves into their culture and their problems, and to feel with them in their pains. Yet this implication of our Lord's example is inescapable. As the Lausanne Covenant puts it: "We affirm that Christ sends his redeemed people into the world as the Father sent him, and that this calls for a similar deep and costly penetration of the world" (para. 6).

The Relation Between Evangelism and Social Action

What, then, should be the relation between evangelism and social action within our total Christian responsibility? If we grant that we have no liberty either to concentrate on evangelism to the exclusion of social concern or to make social activism a substitute for evangelism, we still need to define the relation between the two. Three main ways of doing this have been attempted.

First, some regard social action as a *means to evangelism*. In this case evangelism and the winning of converts are the primary ends in view, but social action is a useful preliminary, an effective means to these ends. In its most blatant form this makes social work (whether food, medicine or education) the sugar on the pill, the bait on the hook, while in its best form it gives to the gospel a credibility it would otherwise lack. In either case the smell of hypocrisy hangs round our philanthropy. A frankly ulterior motive impels us to engage in it. And the result of making our social program the means to another end is that we breed so-called "rice Christians." This is inevitable if we ourselves have been "rice evangelists." They caught the deception from us. No wonder Gandhi said in 1931: "I hold that proselytizing under the cloak of humanitarian work is, to say the least, unhealthy . . . why should I change my religion because a doctor who professes Christianity as his religion has cured me of some disease?"

The second way of relating evangelism and social action is better. It regards social action not as a means to evangelism but as *a manifestation of evangelism*, or at least of the gospel which is being proclaimed. In this case, philanthropy is not attached to evangelism rather artificially from the outside but grows out of it as its natural expression. One might almost say that social action becomes the "sacrament" of evangelism, for it makes the message significantly visible. J. Herman Bavinck in his famous book *An Introduction to the Science of Missions* (Holland, 1954, and Presbyterian & Reformed, 1960) defends this view. Medicine and education are more than "a legitimate and necessary means of creating an opportunity for preaching," he writes, for "if these services are motivated by the proper love and compassion, then they cease to be simply preparation, and at that very moment become preaching" (p.

113). We should not hesitate to agree with this, so far as it goes, for there is a strong precedent for it in the ministry of Jesus. His words and deeds belonged to each other, the words interpreting the deeds and the deeds embodying the words. He did not only announce the good news of the kingdom; he performed visible "signs of the kingdom." If people would not believe his words, he said, then let them believe him "for the sake of the works themselves" (John 14:11).

Bishop John V. Taylor takes a somewhat similar line in his contribution to the Christian Foundations series titled *For All the World* (Hodder & Stoughton, 1966). He writes of a "three-stranded presentation of the Gospel" (p. 43), by which he means that Christians are called to "articulate the gospel . . . through what they say (proclamation), what they are (witness) and what they do (service)" (p. 40). This also is true and finely said. Yet it leaves me uneasy.

For it makes service a subdivision of evangelism, an aspect of the proclamation. I do not deny that good works of love did have an evidential value when performed by Jesus and do have an evidential value when performed by us (cf. Matthew 5:16). But I cannot bring myself to accept that this is their only or even major justification. If it is, then still, and rather self-consciously at that, they are only a means to an end. If good works are visible preaching, then they are expecting a return; but if good works are visible loving, then they are "expecting nothing in return" (Luke 6:35).

This brings me to the third way of stating the relation between evangelism and social action, which I believe to be the truly Christian one, namely, that social action is a *partner of evangelism.* As partners the two belong to each other and yet are independent of each other. Each stands on its own feet in its own right alongside the other. Neither is a means to the other, or even a manifestation of the other. For each is an end in itself. Both are expressions of unfeigned love. As the National Evangelical Anglican Congress at Keele put it in 1967, "Evangelism and compassionate service belong together in the mission of God" (para. 2.20).

The apostle John has helped me to grasp this by these words from his first letter: "If any one has the world's goods and sees his brother in need, yet closes his heart against him, how does God's love abide in him? Little children, let us not love in word or speech but in deed and in truth" (1 John 3:17-18). Here, love in action springs from a twofold situation, first "seeing" a brother in need and second "having" the wherewithal to meet the need. If I do not relate what I "have" to what I "see," I cannot claim to be indwelt by the love of God. Further, this principle applies whatever the nature of the seen need. I may see spiritual need (sin, guilt, lostness) and have the gospel knowledge to meet it.

Or the need I see may be disease or ignorance or bad housing, and I may have the medical, educational or social expertise to relieve it. To see need and to possess the remedy compels love to act, and whether the action will be evangelistic or social, or indeed political, depends on what we "see" and what we "have."

This does not mean that words and works, evangelism and social action, are such inseparable partners that all of us must engage in both all the time. Situations vary, and so do Christian callings. As for situations, there will be times when a person's eternal destiny is the most urgent consideration, for we must not forget that men without Christ are perishing. But there will certainly be other times when a person's material need is so pressing that he would not be able to hear the gospel if we shared it with him. The man who fell among robbers needed above all else at that moment oil and bandages for his wounds, not evangelistic tracts in his pockets! Similarly, in the words of a missionary in Nairobi quoted by Bishop John Taylor, "a hungry man has no ears" (p. 37). If our enemy is hungry, our biblical mandate is not to evangelize him but to feed him (Romans 12:20)! Then too there is a diversity of Christian callings, and every Christian should be faithful to his own calling. The doctor must not neglect the practice of medicine for evangelism, nor should the evangelist be distracted from the ministry of the word by the ministry of tables, as the apostles quickly discovered (Acts 6).

The Great Commandment

Let me return now to the Great Commission. I have tried to argue that its Johannine form, according to which the church's mission is to be modeled on the Son's, implies that we are sent into the world to serve, and that the humble service we are to render will include for us as it did for Christ both words and works, a concern for the hunger and for the sickness of both body and soul, in other words, both evangelistic and social activity. But supposing someone remains convinced that the Great Commission relates exclusively to evangelism, what then?

I venture to say that sometimes, perhaps because it was the last instruction Jesus gave us before returning to the Father, we give the Great Commission too prominent a place in our Christian thinking. Please do not misunderstand me. I firmly believe that the whole church is under obligation to obey its Lord's commission to take the gospel to all nations. But I am also concerned that we should not regard this as the only instruction which Jesus left us. He also quoted Leviticus 19:18, "you shall love your neighbor as yourself" (Matthew 22:39), called it the second and great commandment (second in importance only to the supreme command to love God with all our being), and elaborated on it in the Sermon on the Mount. There he insisted that in God's vocabulary our neighbor includes our enemy, and that to love means to "do good," that is, to give ourselves actively and constructively to serve our neighbor's welfare.

Here then are two instructions of Jesus—a great commandment, "love your neighbor," and a great commission, "go and make disciples." What is the relation between the two? Some of us behave as if we thought them identical, so that if we share the gospel with somebody, we consider we have completed our responsibility to love him. But no. The Great Commission neither explains, nor exhausts, nor supersedes the Great Commandment. What it does is to add to the requirement of neighbor-love and neighbor-service a new and urgent Christian dimension. If we truly love our neighbor, we shall without doubt share with him the good news of Jesus.

How can we possibly claim to love him if we know the gospel but keep it from him? Equally, however, if we truly love our neighbor, we shall not stop with evangelism. Our neighbor is neither a bodiless soul that we should love only his soul, nor a soulless body that we should care for its welfare alone, nor even a body-soul isolated from society. God created man, who is my neighbor, a body-soul-in-community. Therefore, if we love our neighbor as God made him, we must inevitably be concerned for his total welfare—the good of his soul, his body and his community. Moreover, it is this vision of man as a social being, as well as a psycho-somatic being, which obliges us to add a *political* dimension to our social concern. Humanitarian activity cares for the casualties of a sick society. We should be concerned with preventive medicine or community health as well, which means the quest for better social structures in which peace, dignity, freedom and justice are secured for all men. And there is no reason why, in pursuing this quest, we should not join hands with all men of good will, even if they are not Christians.

To sum up, we are sent into the world, like Jesus, to serve. For this is the natural expression of our love for our neighbors. We love. We go. We serve. And in this we have (or should have) no ulterior motive. True, the gospel lacks visibility if we merely preach it, and lacks credibility if we who preach it are interested only in souls and have no concern about the welfare of people's bodies, situations and communities. Yet the reason for our acceptance of social responsibility is not primarily in order to give the gospel either a visibility or a credibility it would otherwise lack, but rather simple

MISSION

uncomplicated compassion. Love has no need to justify itself. It merely expresses itself in service wherever it sees need.

Mission, then, is not a word for everything the church does. "The church is mission" sounds fine, but it is an overstatement. For the church is a worshiping as well as a serving community, and although worship and service belong together they are not to be confused. Nor, as we have seen, does "mission" cover everything God does in the world. For God the Creator is constantly active in his world in providence, in common grace and in judgment, quite apart from the purposes for which he has sent his Son, his Spirit and his church into the world. "Mission" describes rather everything the church is sent into the world to do. "Mission" embraces the church's double vocation of service to be "the salt of the earth" and "the light of the world." For Christ *sends* his people into the earth to be its salt, and sends his people into the world to be its light (Matthew 5:13-16).

Practical Implications

In conclusion, it may be helpful to consider what the realistic outworkings of this understanding of "mission" are likely to be. Evangelical Christians are now repenting of the former pietism which tended to keep us insulated from the secular world, and are accepting that we have a social as well as an evangelistic responsibility. But what will this mean in practice? I would like to explore three areas—vocational, local and national.

I begin with vocation, by which I mean a Christian's lifework. We often given the impression that if a young

Christian is really keen for Christ, he or she will undoubtedly become a foreign missionary, that if he is not quite as keen as that he will stay at home and become a pastor, that if he lacks the dedication to be a pastor, he will no doubt serve as a doctor or a teacher, while those who end up in social work or the media or (worst of all) in politics are not far removed from serious backsliding! It seems to me urgent to gain a truer perspective in this matter of vocation. Jesus Christ calls all his disciples to "ministry," that is, to service. He himself is the Servant par excellence, and he calls us to be servants too. This much then is certain: if we are Christians, we must spend our lives in the service of God and others.

The only difference between us lies in the nature of the service we are called to render. Some are indeed called to be missionaries, evangelists or pastors, and others to the great professions of law, education, medicine and the social sciences. But others are called to commerce, to industry and farming, to accountancy and banking, to local government or parliament, and to the mass media, while there are still many women who find their vocation in homemaking and parenthood without pursuing an independent career as well. In all these spheres, and many others besides, it is possible for Christians to interpret their lifework Christianly, and to see it neither as a necessary evil (necessary, that is, for survival), nor even as a useful place in which to evangelize or make money for evangelism, but as their Christian vocation, as the way Christ has called them to spend their lives in his service. Further, a part of their calling will be to seek to maintain Christ's standards of justice, righteousness, honesty, human

29

dignity and compassion in a society which no longer accepts them.

When any community deteriorates, the blame should be attached where it belongs: not to the community which is going bad but to the church which is failing in its responsibility as salt to stop it going bad. And the salt will be effective only if it permeates society, only if Christians learn again the wide diversity of divine callings, and if many penetrate deeply into secular society in order to serve Christ there.

To this end I would personally like to see the appointment of Christian vocation officers who would visit schools, colleges and churches not to recruit for the pastorate only but to set before young people the exciting variety of opportunities available today for serving Christ and their fellow human beings. I would also like to see regular vocation conferences, not *missionary* conferences only which accord the top priority to becoming a crosscultural missionary, nor *ministry* conferences which concentrate on the ordained pastorate, but *mission* conferences which portray the biblical breadth of the mission of God, apply it to today's world and challenge young people to give their lives unreservedly to service in some aspect of the Christian mission.

A second application concerns the local church. Here again our tendency has been to see the church as a worshiping and witnessing community, its responsibility to the parish or district being largely restricted to evangelistic witness. But if the local church is "sent" into its area as the Father sent the Son into the world, its mission of service is wider than evangelism. Once the local church as a whole recognizes and accepts this fuller dimension of its responsibility, it is ready for a further truth. Although all Christians are called in general terms to both kinds of service, to witness to Christ and to play the good Samaritan when the opportunity presents itself, not all Christians are called either to give their lives to both or to spend all their spare time in both.

It is clearly impossible for everybody to do everything which needs to be done. Therefore there must be specialization according to the gifts and calling of Christ. Some members of the local church are without doubt gifted for evangelism and called to evangelism. But can we now say with equal conviction that Christ's gifts and calling to others point rather in a social direction? Can we now liberate ourselves from the man-made bondage (for that is what it is) of supposing that every really keen Christian will devote all his spare time to some soul-winning enterprise? Surely the biblical doctrine of the body of Christ, with different members gifted to fulfill different functions, should be enough to give us this larger freedom?

Once this principle has been welcomed, it should be possible for groups of concerned Christians in every congregation to coalesce into a variety of "study and action groups." For example, one might concentrate on house-to-house visitation, another on the evangelistic penetration of some particular unreached section (e.g., a hostel or youth club, a college or coffee bar), another on community relations among immigrants, another on setting up a housing association to help the homeless, another on visiting old folk or the sick, or helping the handicapped, while others might address themselves to wider socioethical or sociopolitical questions such as abortion (if there is an abortion clinic in the parish) or labor relations (if the parish is industrial) or permissiveness and censorship (if local pornographic shops or cinemas are an offense in the neighborhood). I have deliberately used the expression "study and action groups" because we Christians have a tendency to pontificate from a position of ignorance, and we need to grapple with the complexities of our subject before recommending some course of responsible action, whether evangelistic or social or both, to the church council.

My third example of taking seriously the broader biblical understanding of mission brings us to the national scene. Although initiatives ought to be taken locally, it would be a considerable strength to parochial study and action groups if some kind of national network could be established. At the moment in England national organizations exist for youth work (e.g., Pathfinders and CYFA), for foreign missions (the various missionary societies), for overseas relief and development (e.g., TEAR Fund), and for one or two other purposes, but not for mission in the broader sense. Church of England Evangelical Council and the Evangelical Alliance have begun talking about a think tank which might seek to develop a national strategy for the evangelization of Britain. I hope it will root itself in local situations by linking evangelistic "study and action groups" with one another. Perhaps it should also be concerned not only for evangelism but for mission in the wider sense. Or maybe this is a job for the Shaftesbury Project or the Festival of Light or some other organization.

Out of such a network of local groups it seems to me that one or two influential central groups could arise. We hear a lot today about "alienation," not just in the classical economic sense developed by Marx, but in the more general sense of powerlessness. Jimmy Reid, the Marxist dockside leader who became rector of Glasgow University in 1972, spoke about this during his installation address: "Alienation is the cry of men who feel themselves to be the victims of blind economic forces beyond their control, . . . the frustration of ordinary people excluded from the processes of decision-making." And it is true. Many people feel themselves to be helpless slaves of "the system." But Christians have no business to acquiesce in a feeling of helplessness. I find myself in agreement with Barbara Ward who, in what to me was the most scintillating speech at Uppsala, said: "Christians straddle the whole spectrum of rich nations, and therefore Christians are a lobby, or can be a lobby, of incomprehensible importance." She was talking particularly about development aid.

If we can accept this broader concept of mission as Christian service in the world comprising both evangelism and social action—a concept which is laid upon us by the model of our Savior's mission in the world—then Christians could under God make a far greater impact on society, an impact commensurate with our numerical strength and with the radical demands of the commission of Christ.

CPSIA information can be obtained
at www.ICGtesting.com
Printed in the USA
BVHW032111140619
551101BV00001B/4/P

9 781573 835787